ADULTS COLORING BOOK

This Book
Belongs To

____

Coloring Creator

ISBN-13: 978-1978267626

COLOR TEST PAGE

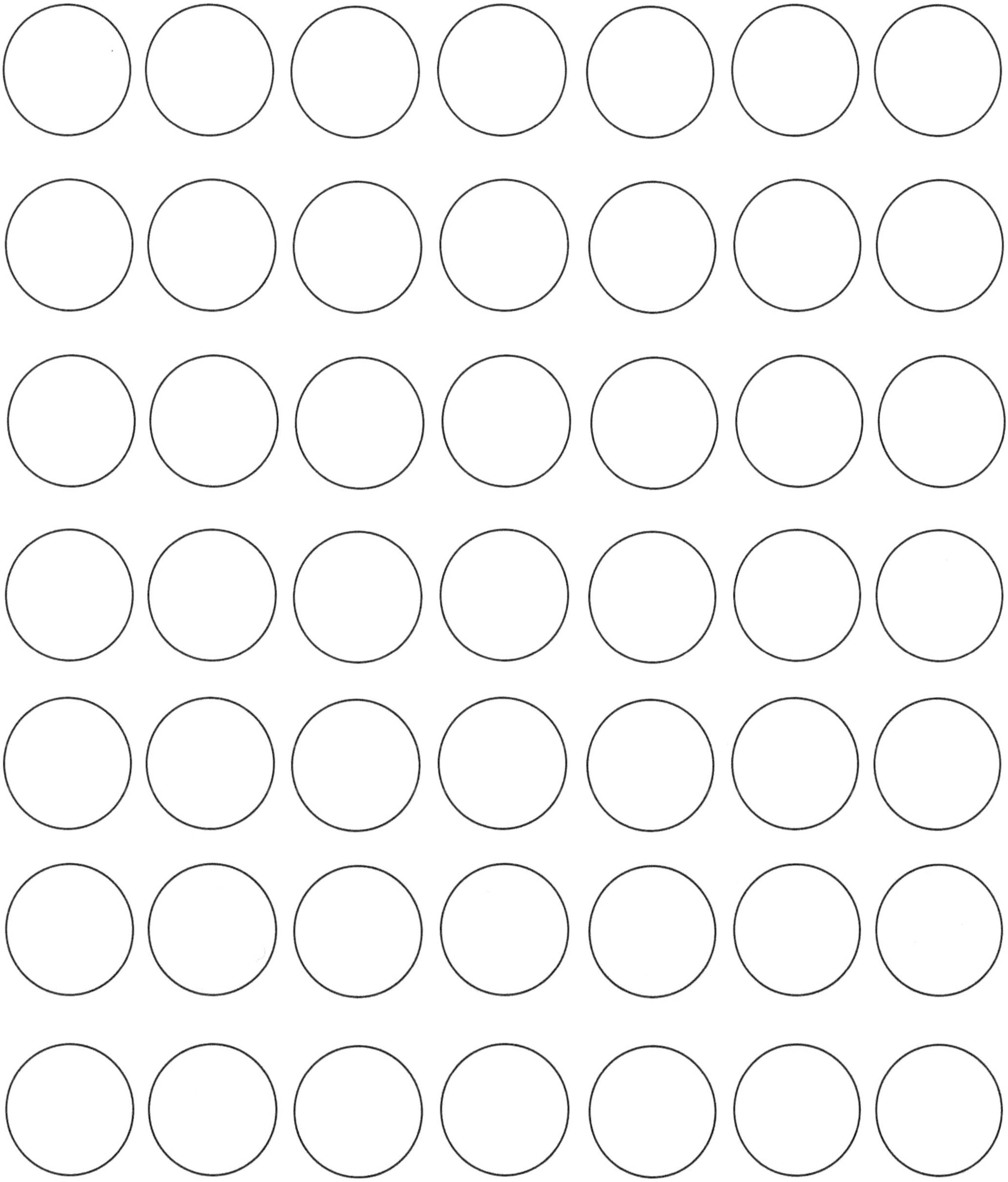

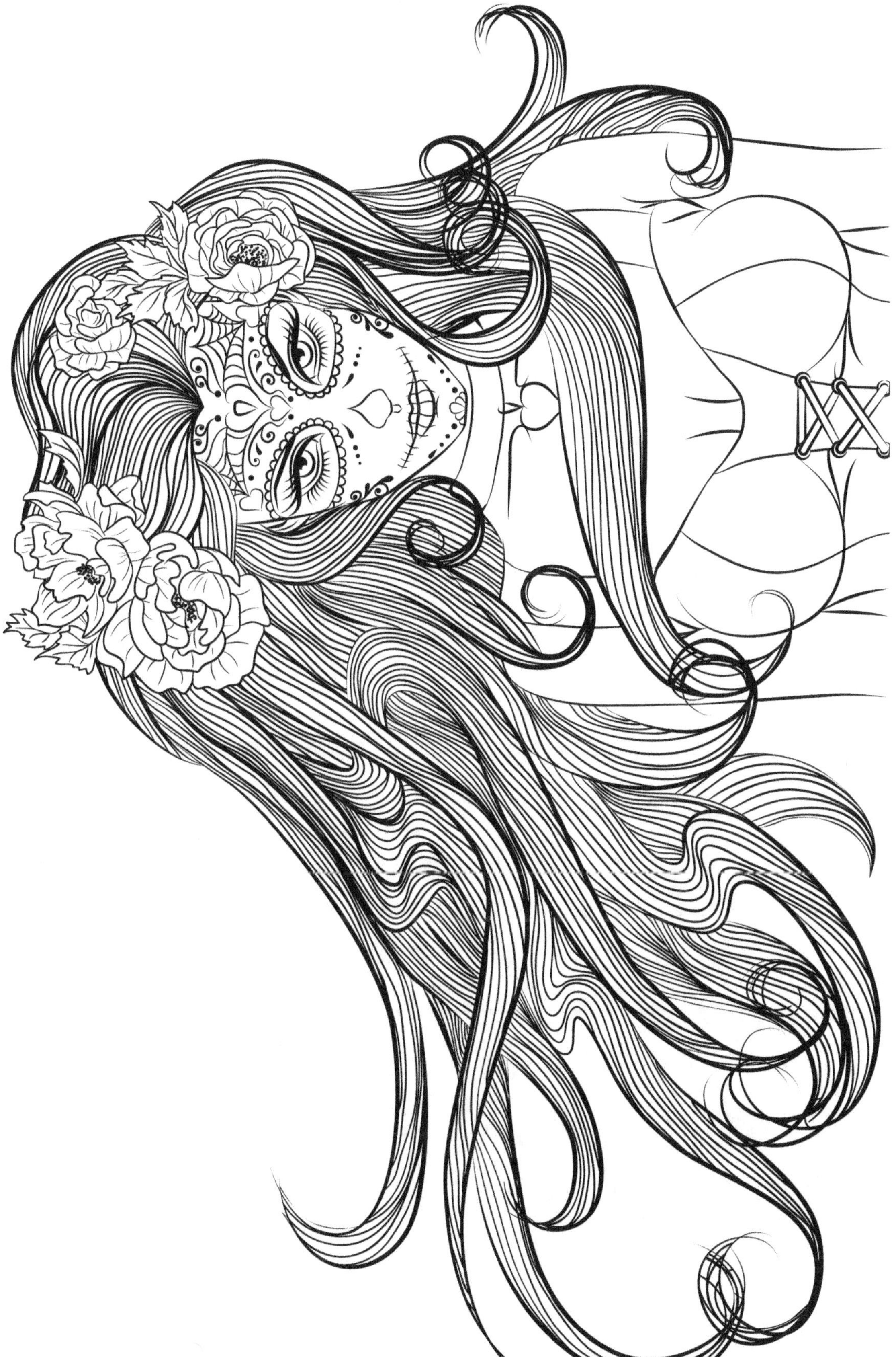

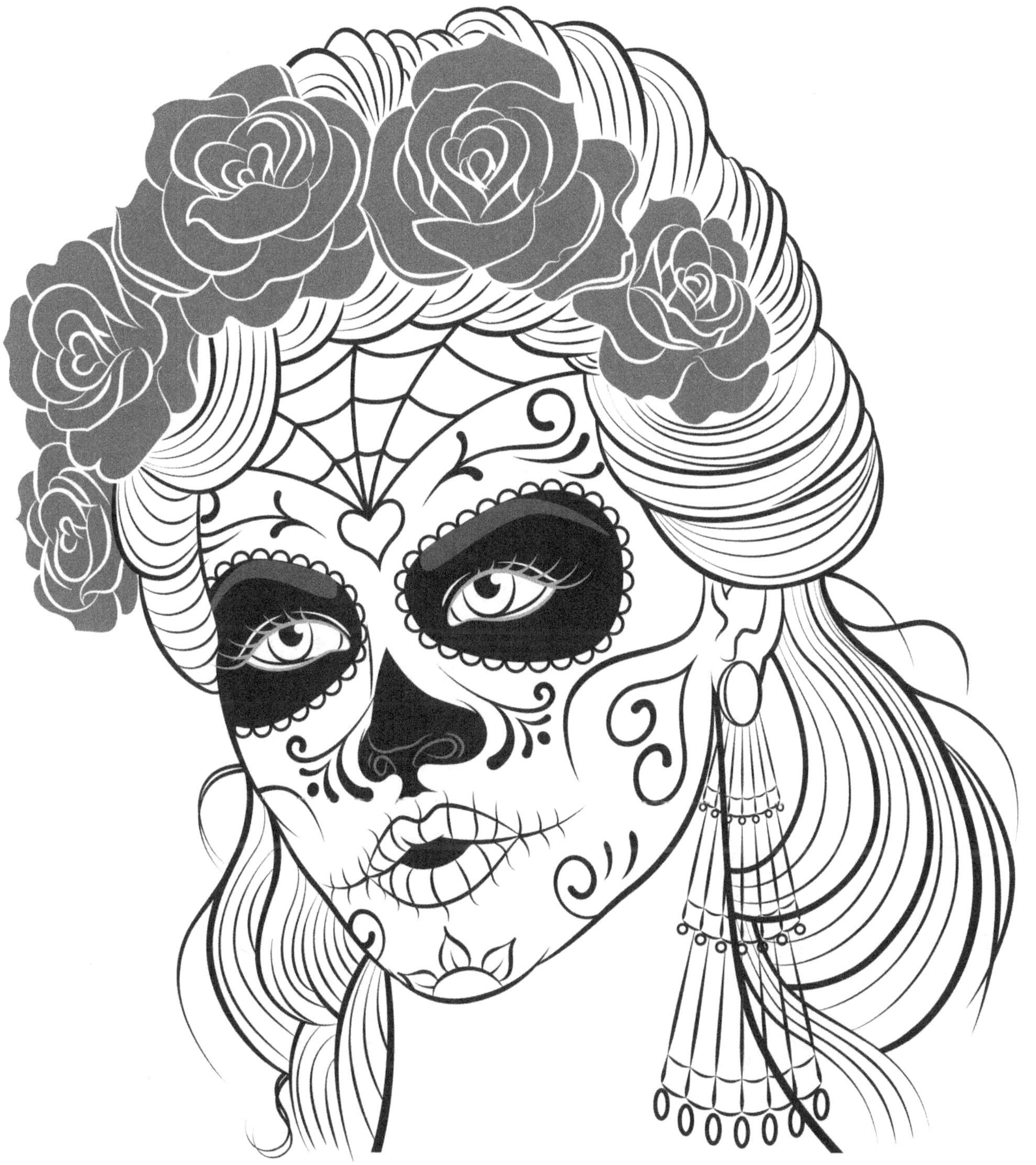

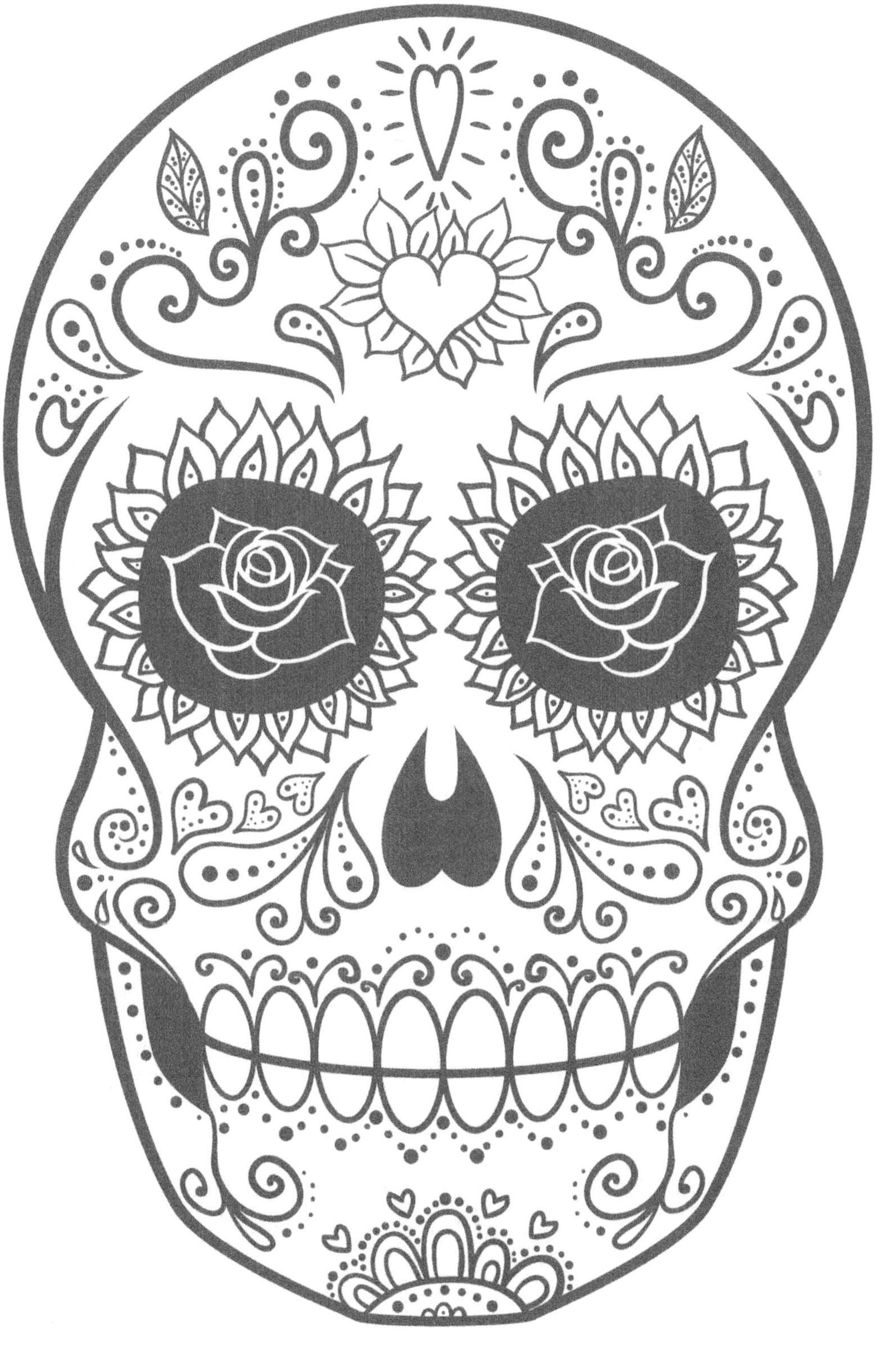

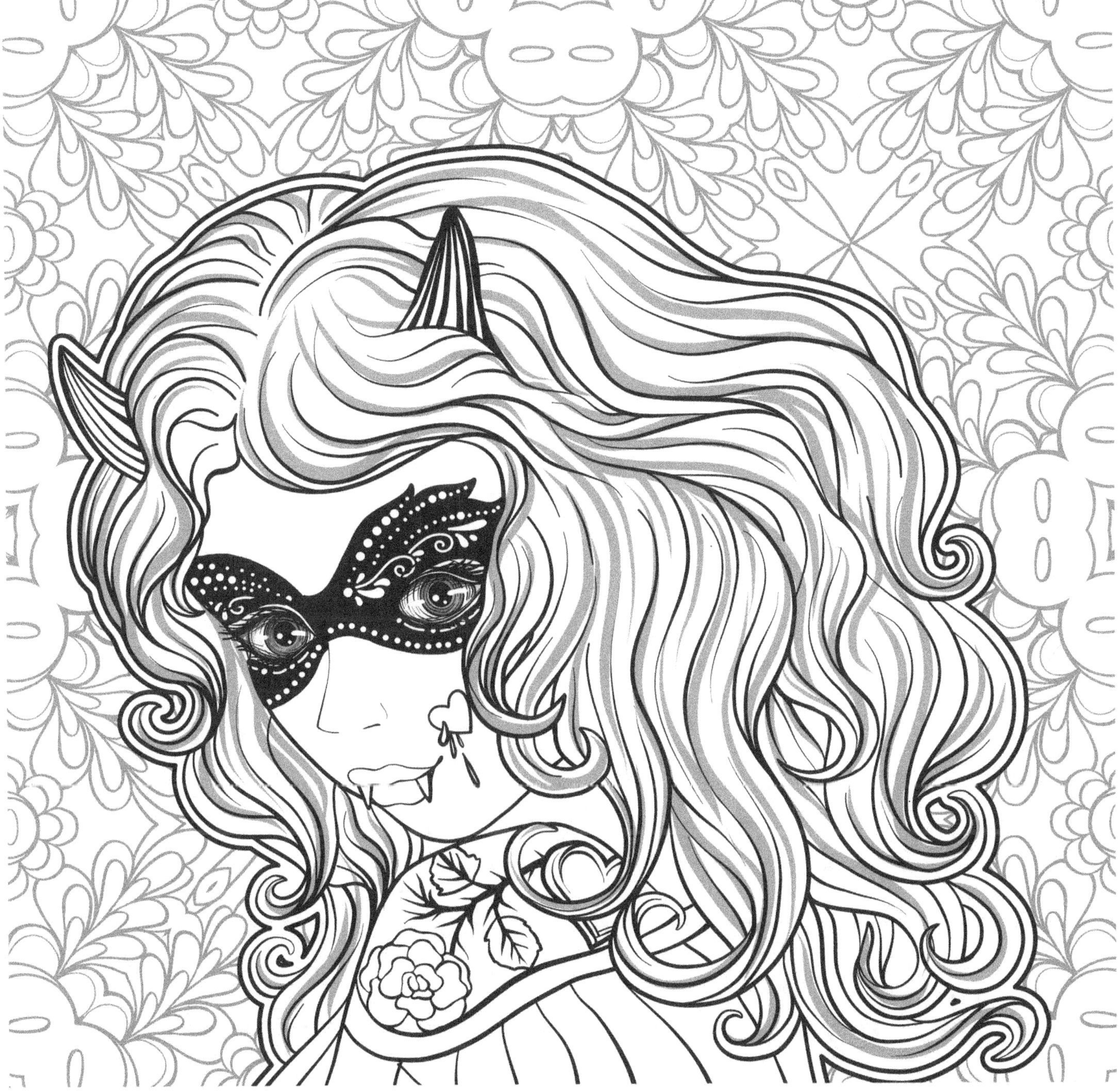

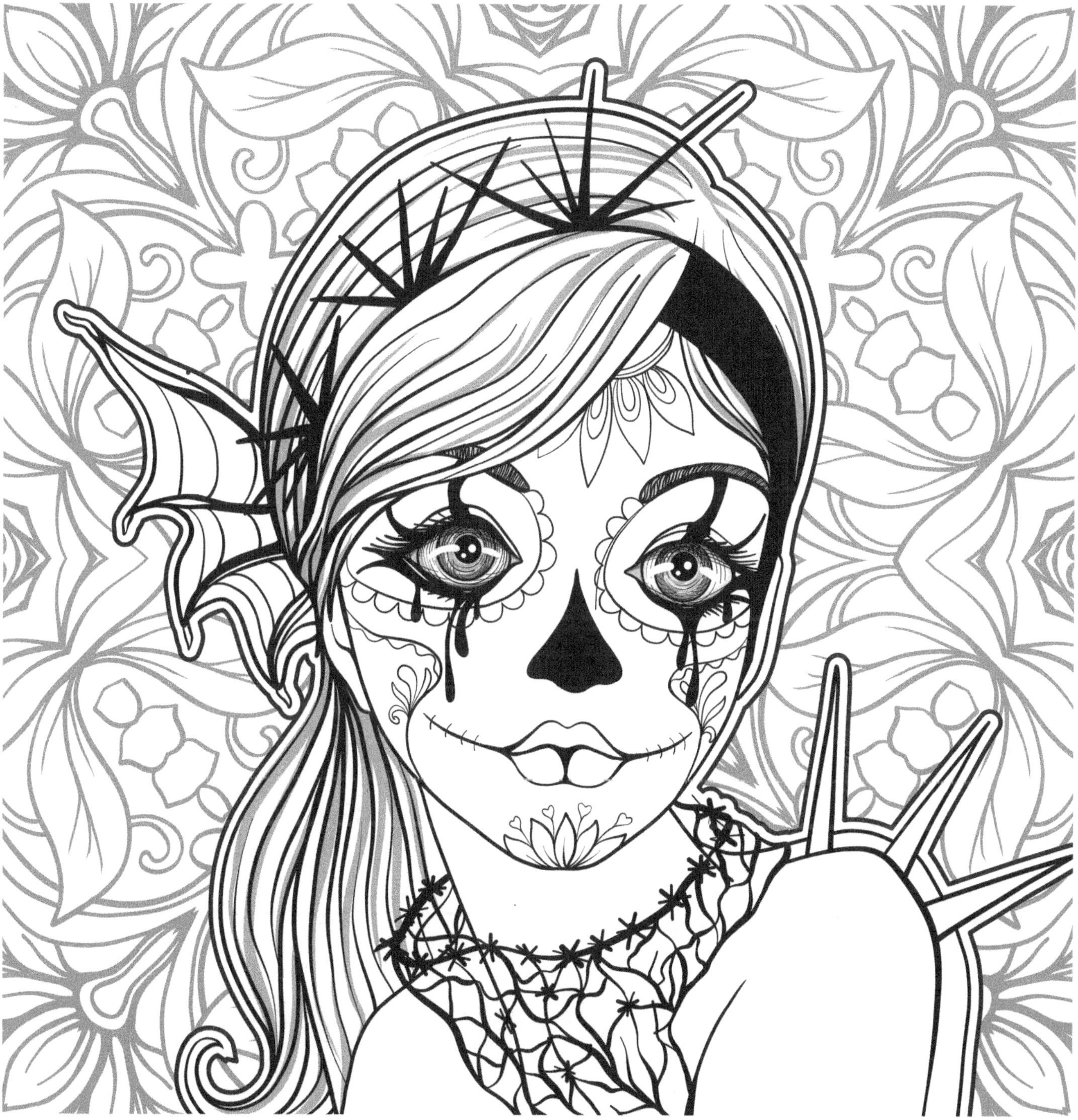

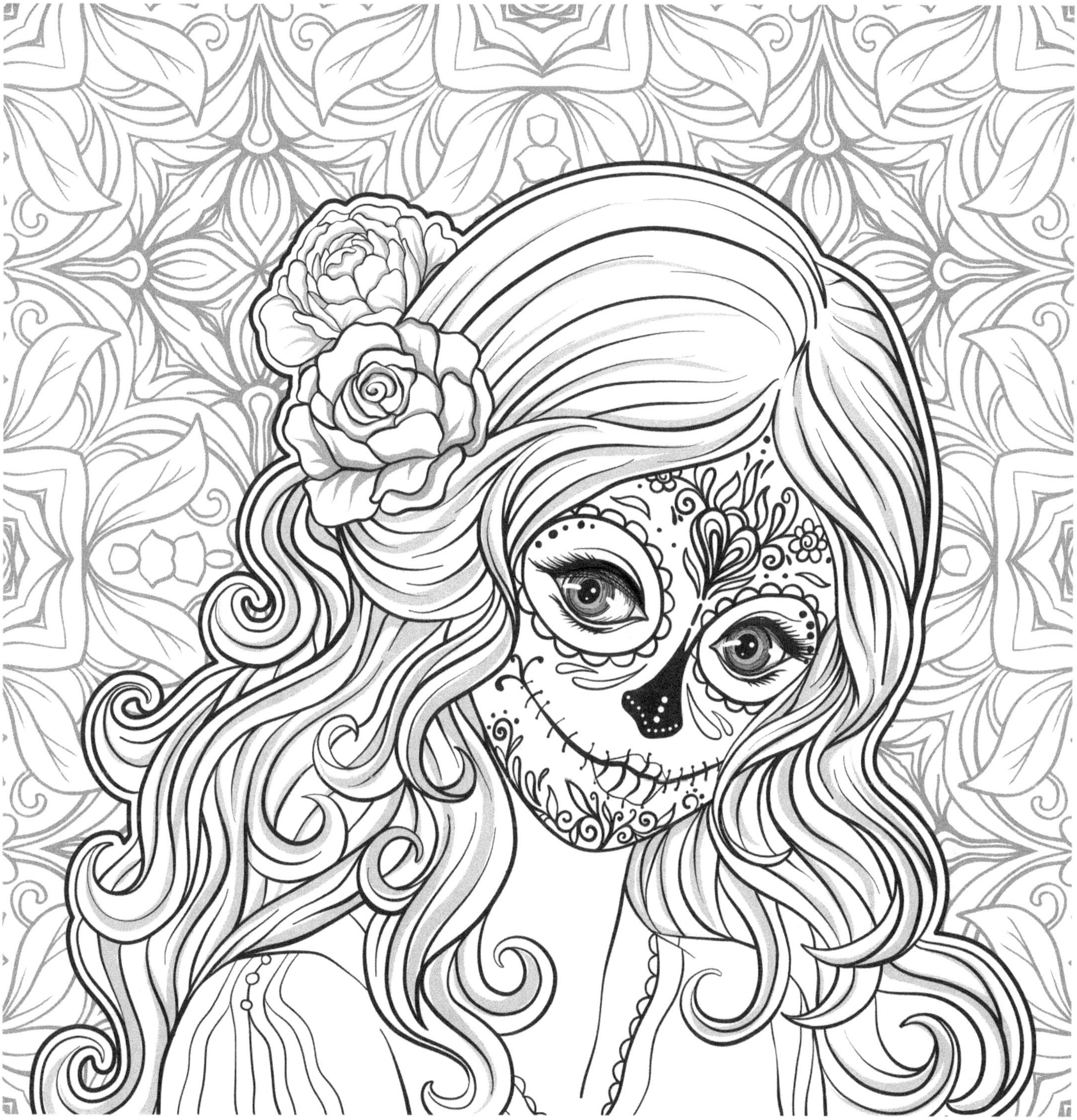

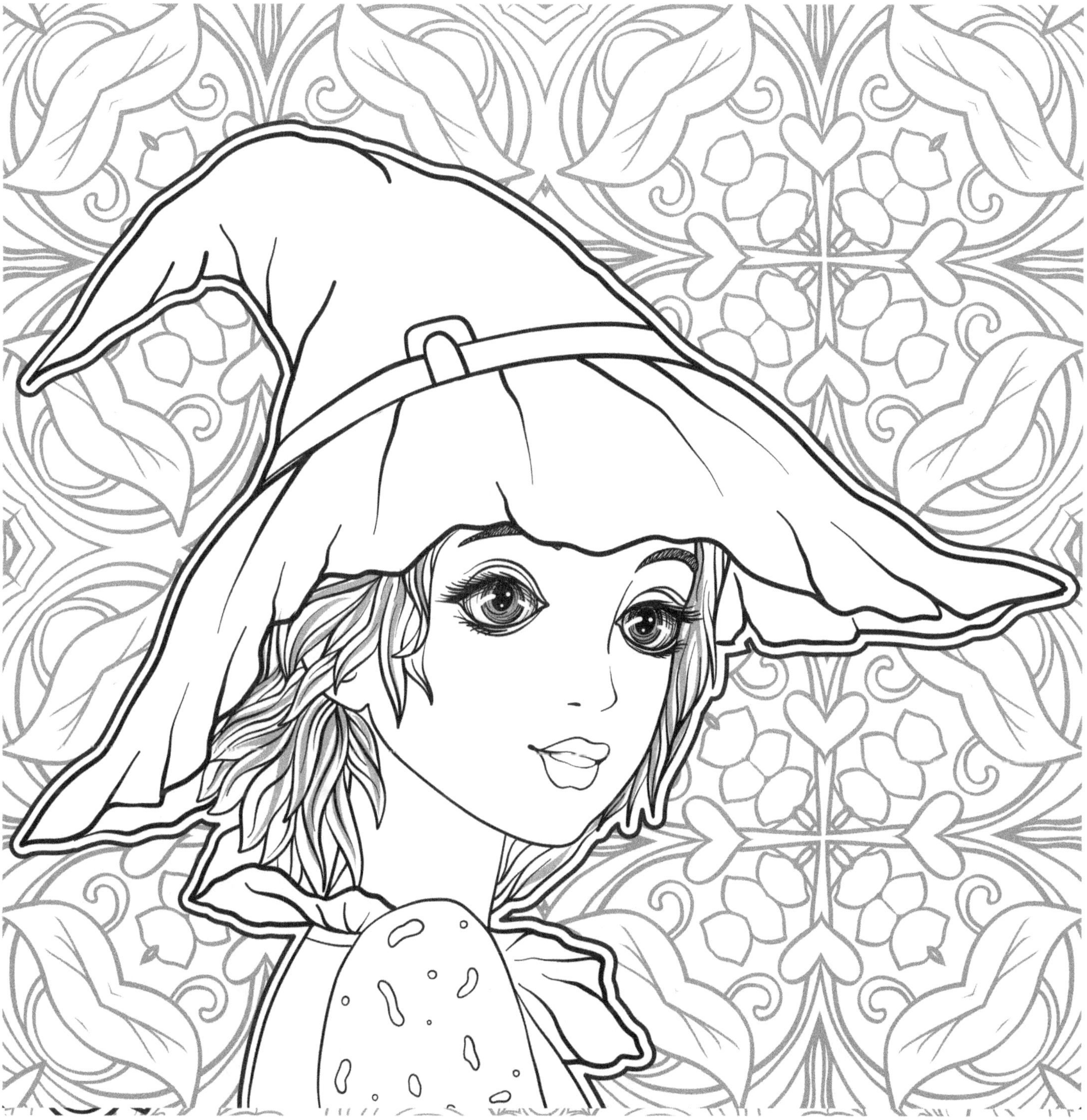

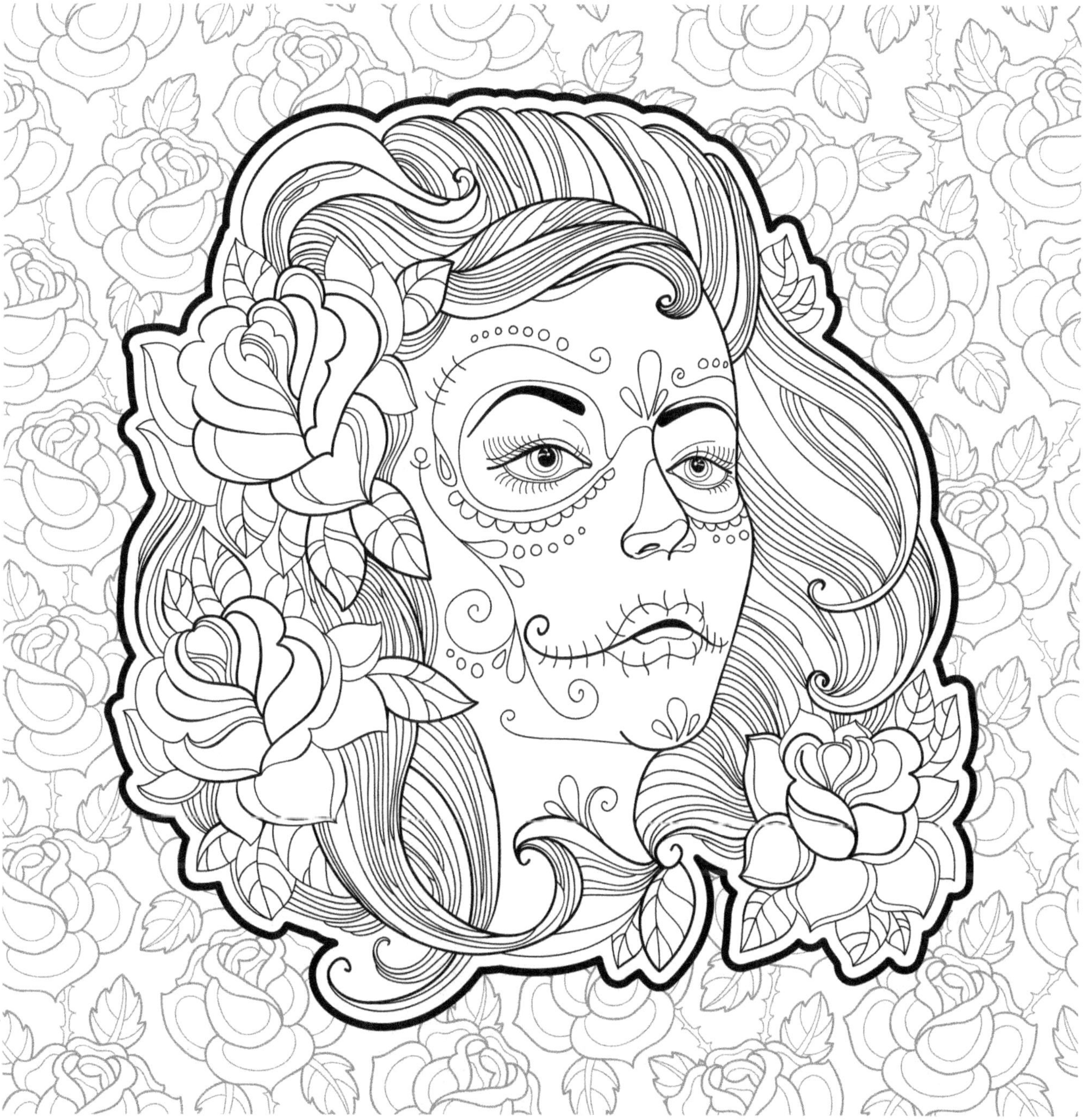

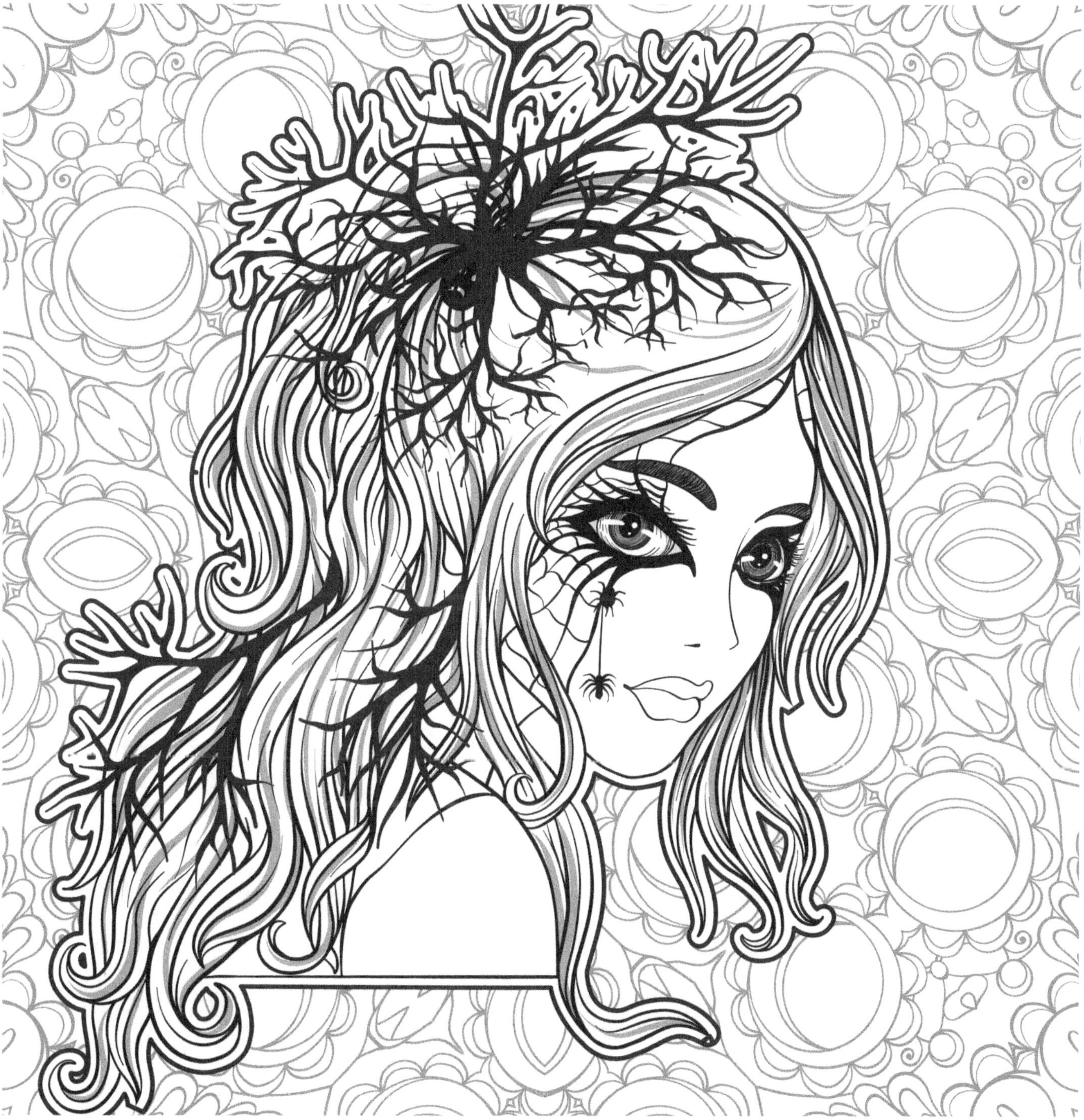

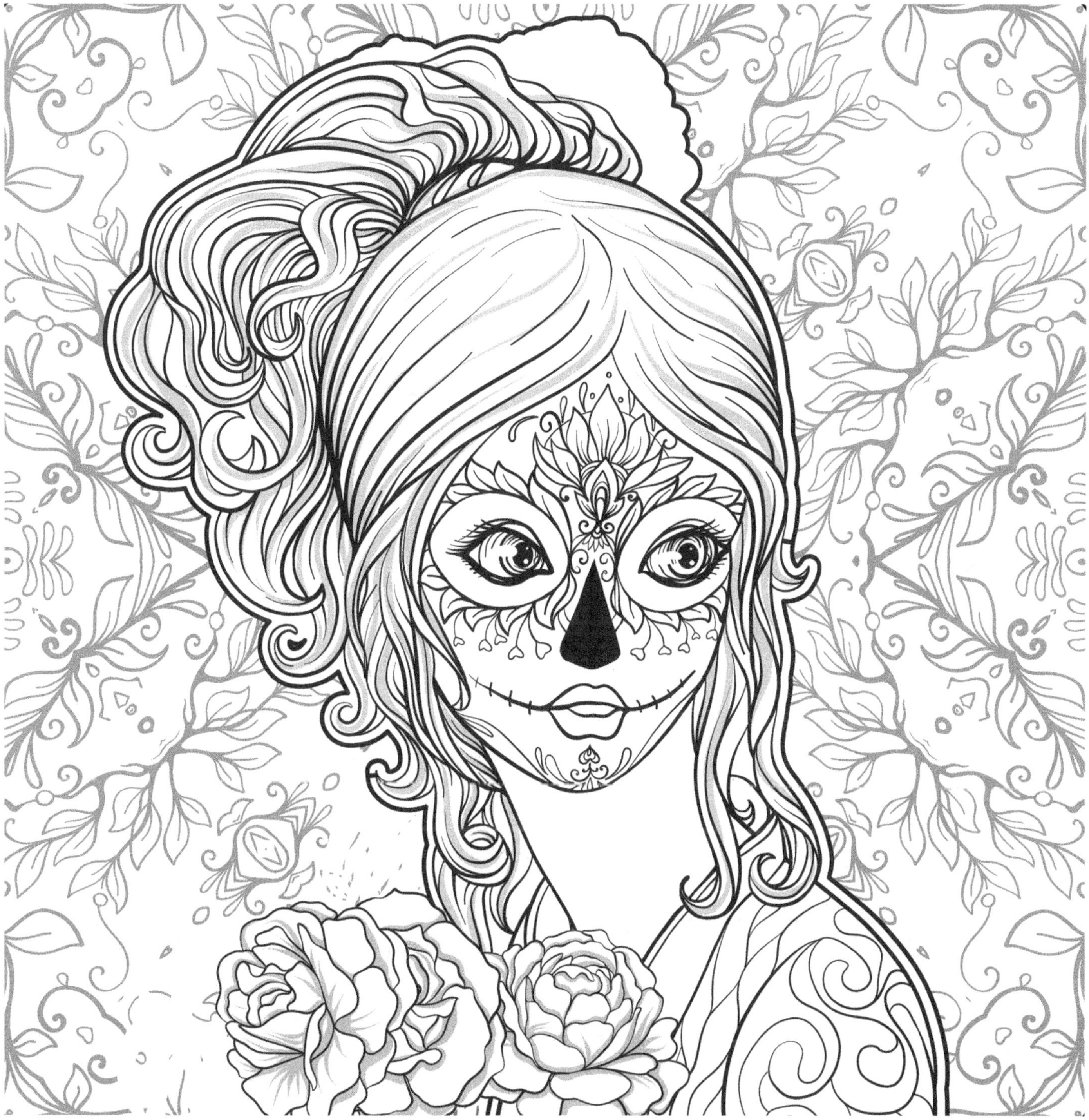

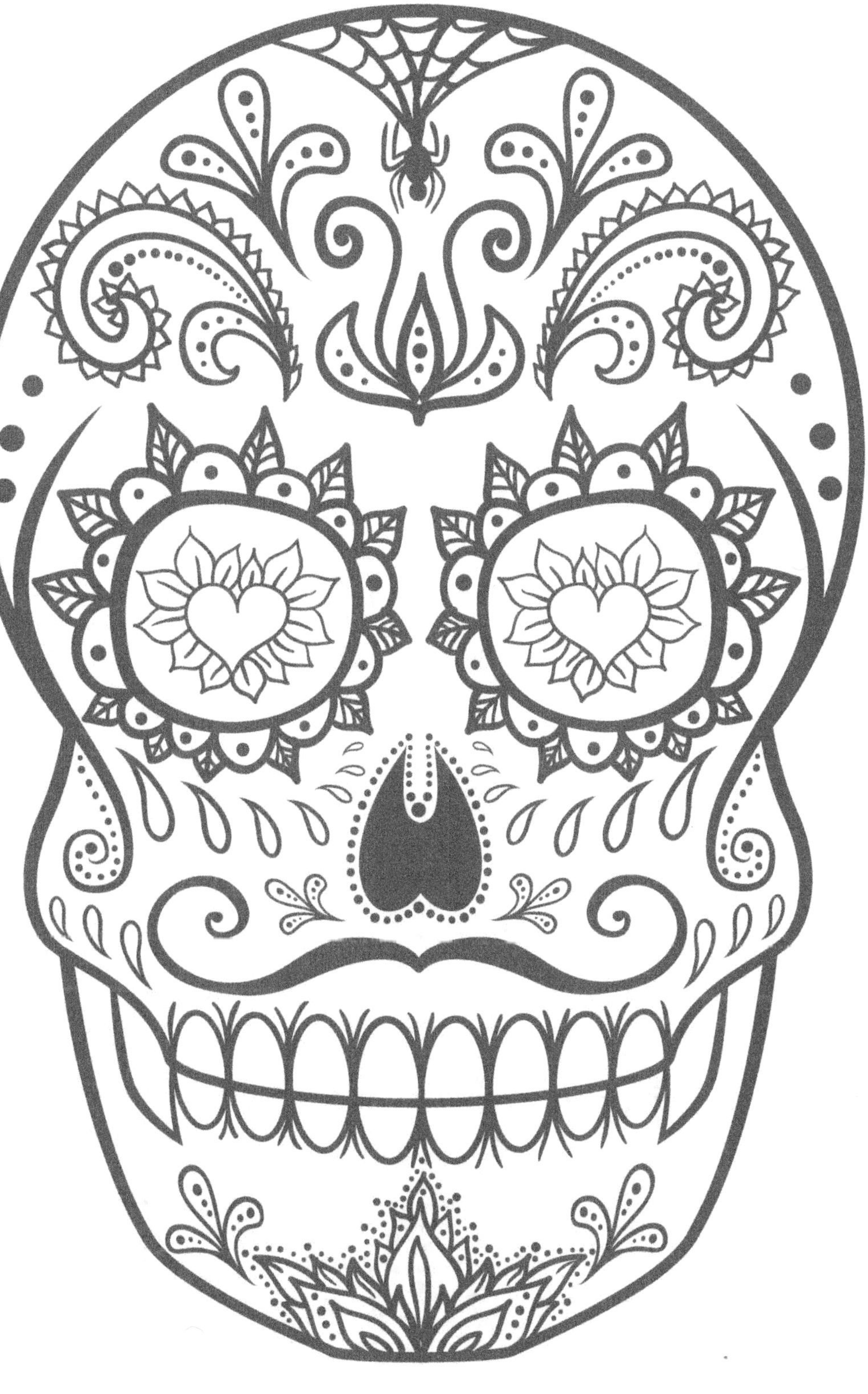

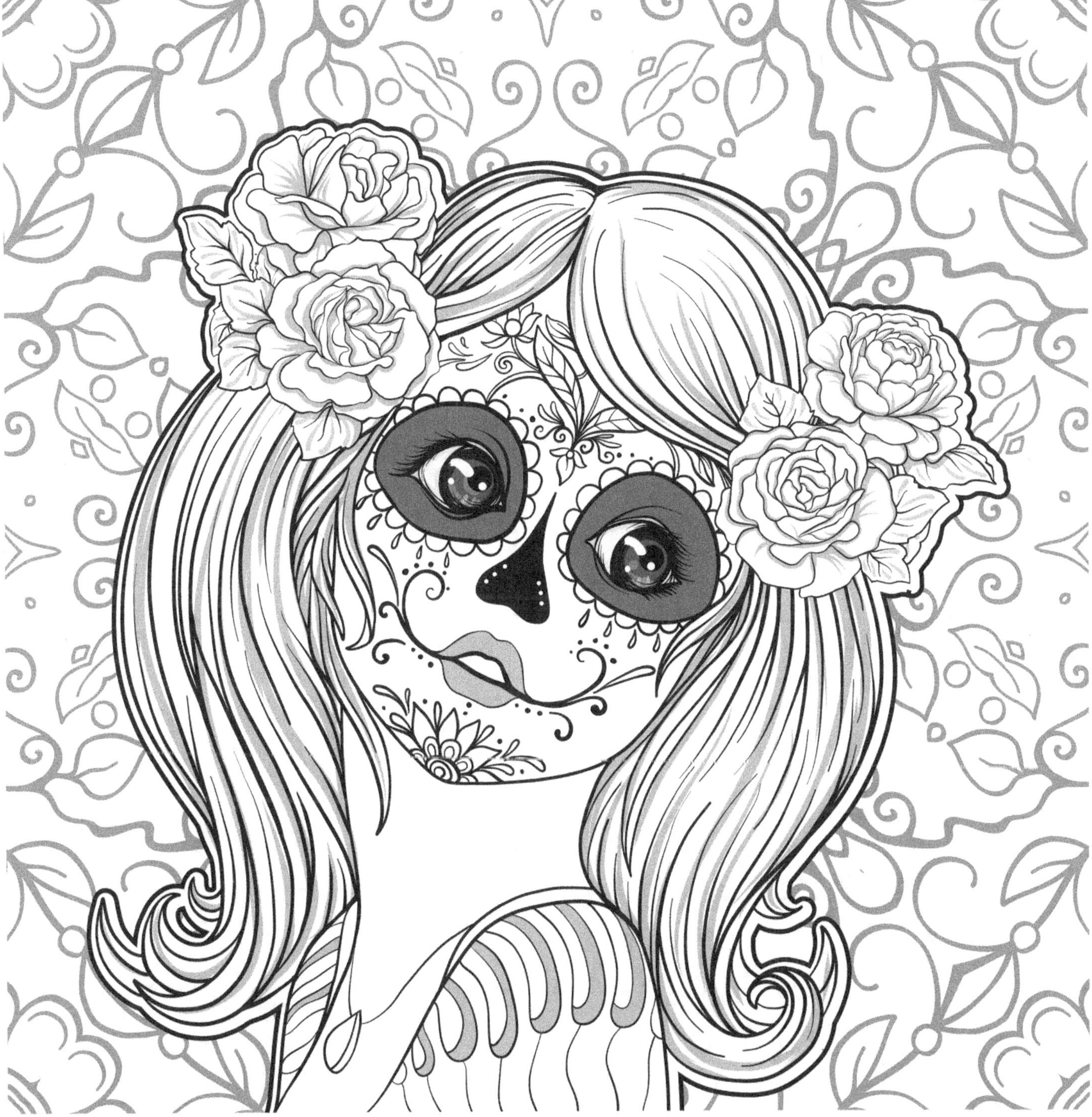

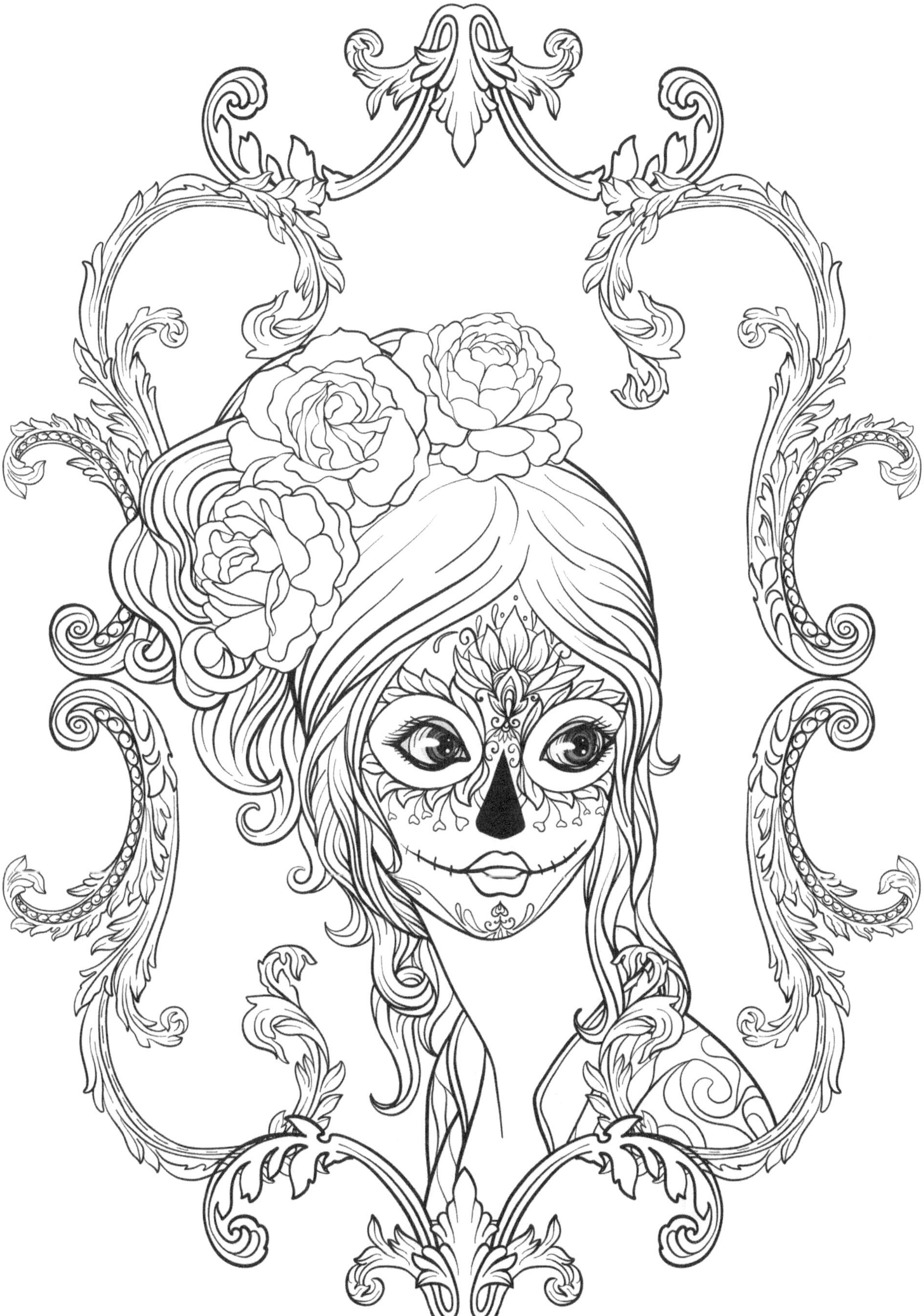

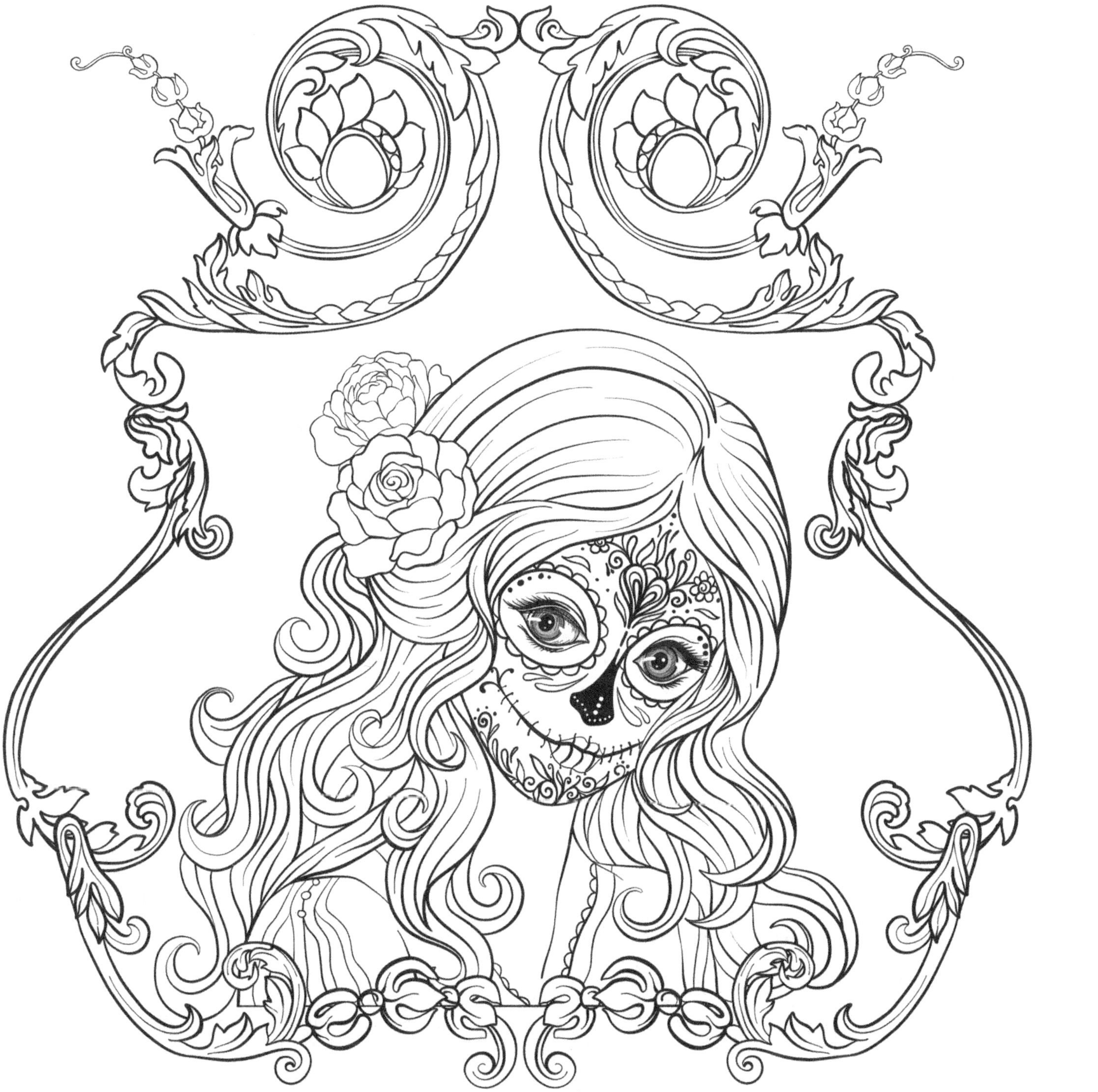

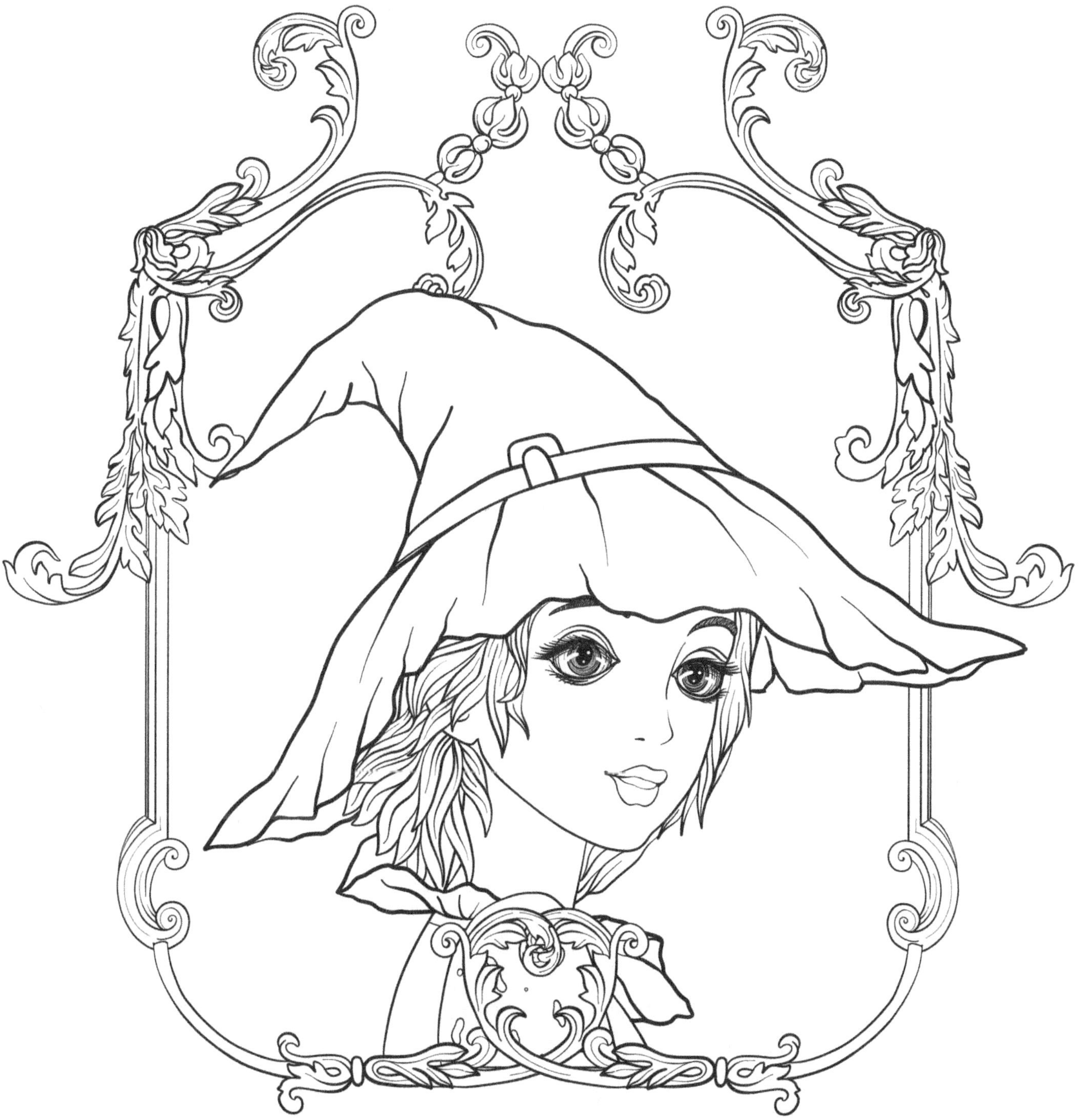

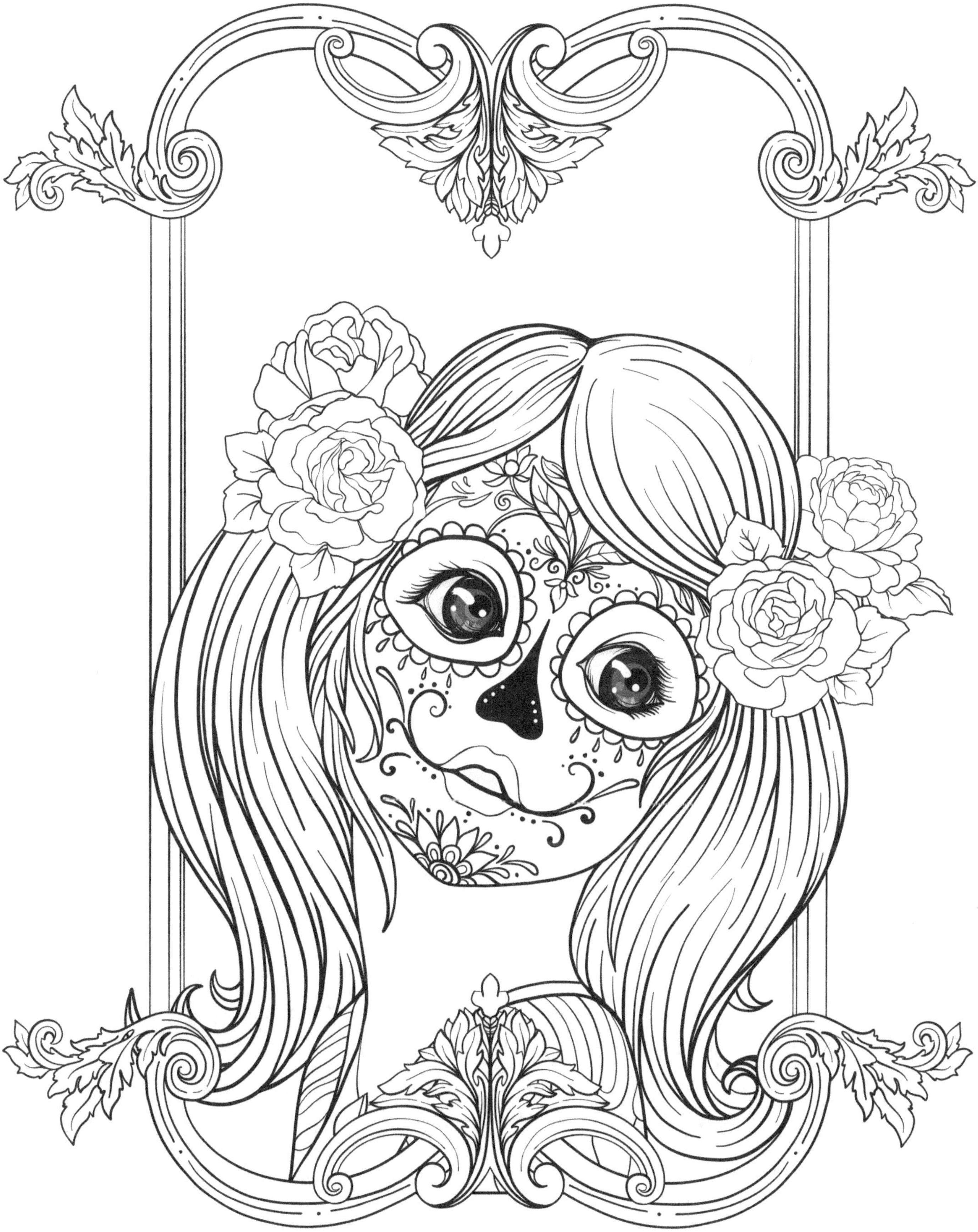

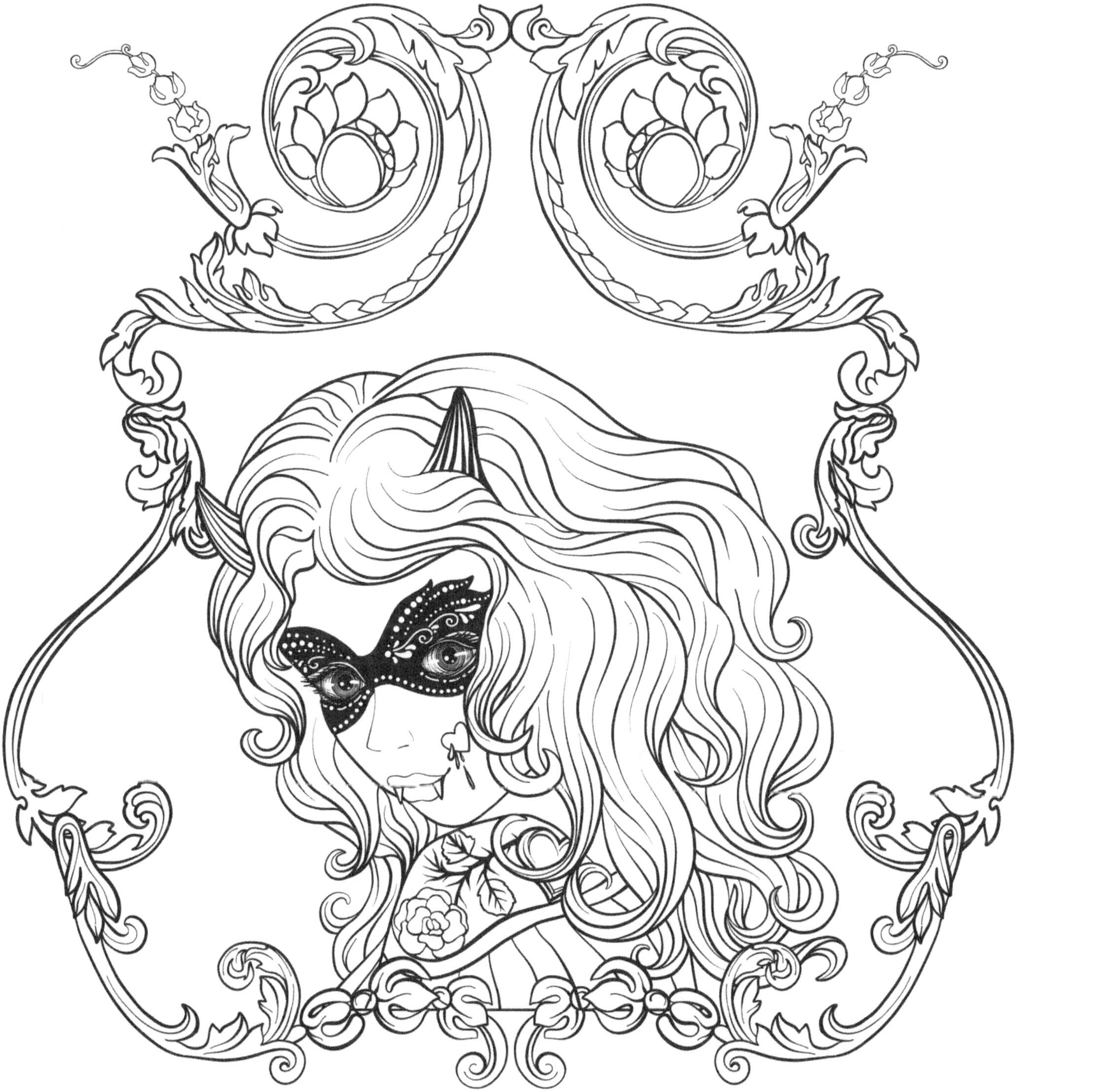

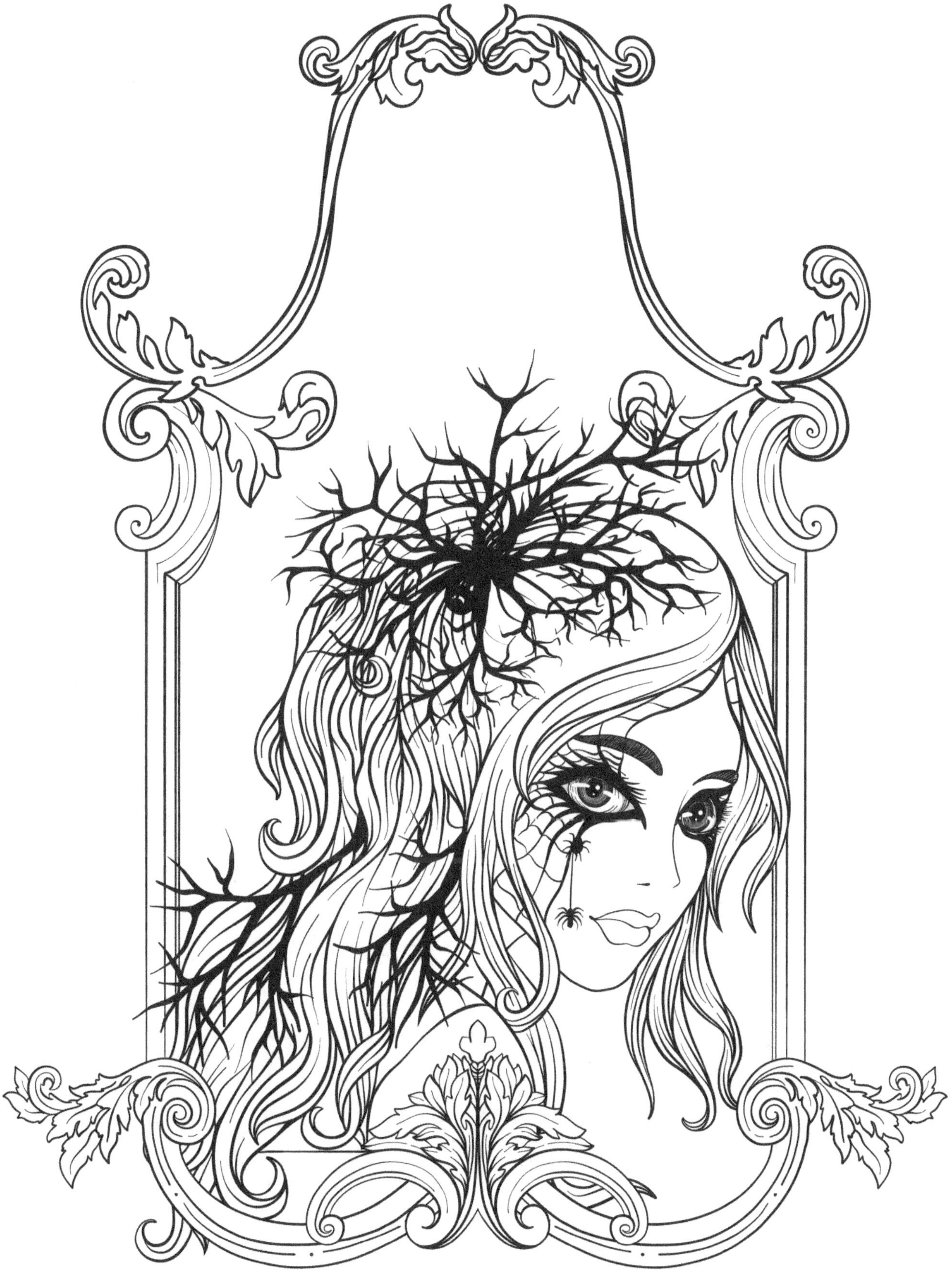

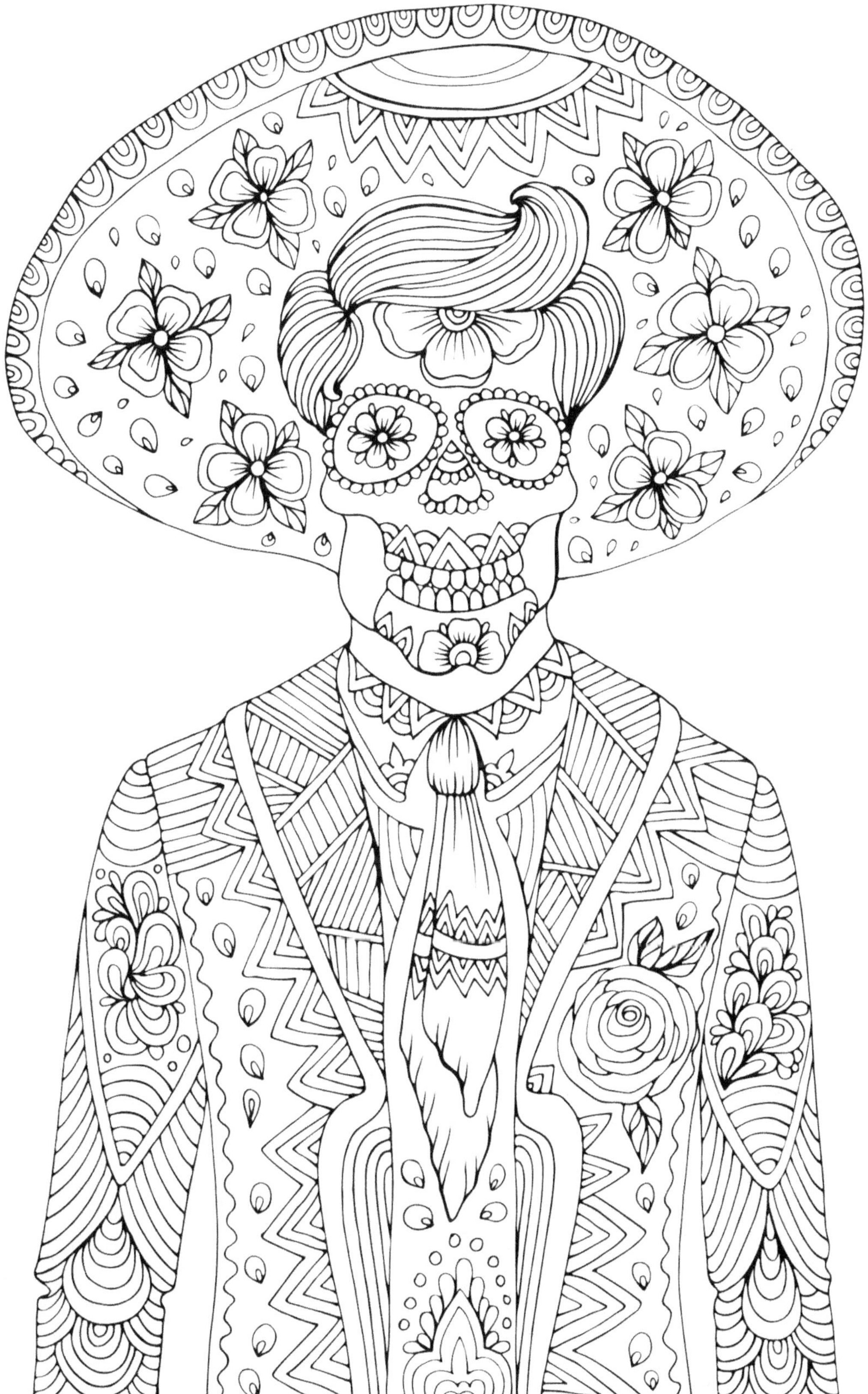

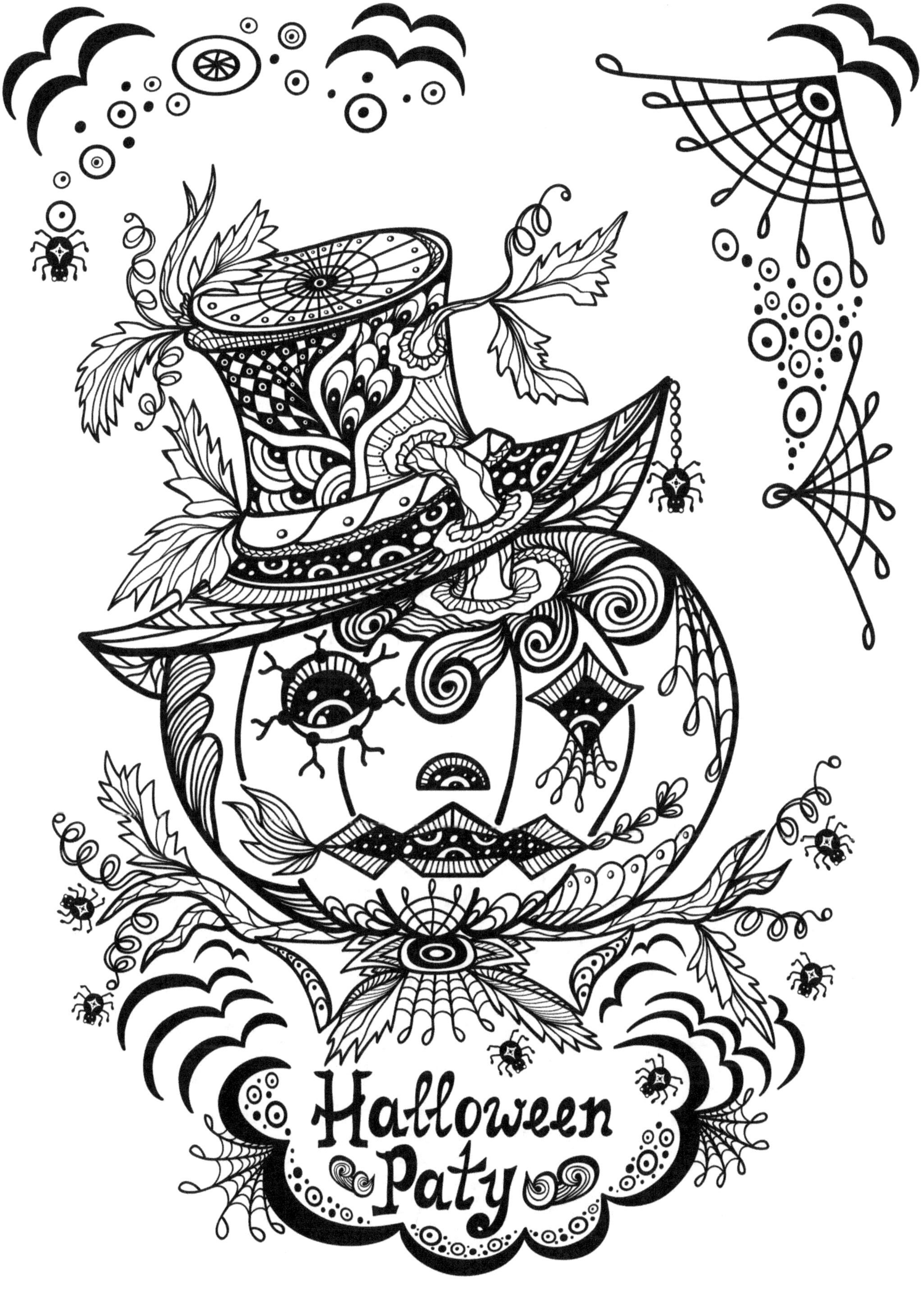
Halloween
Paty

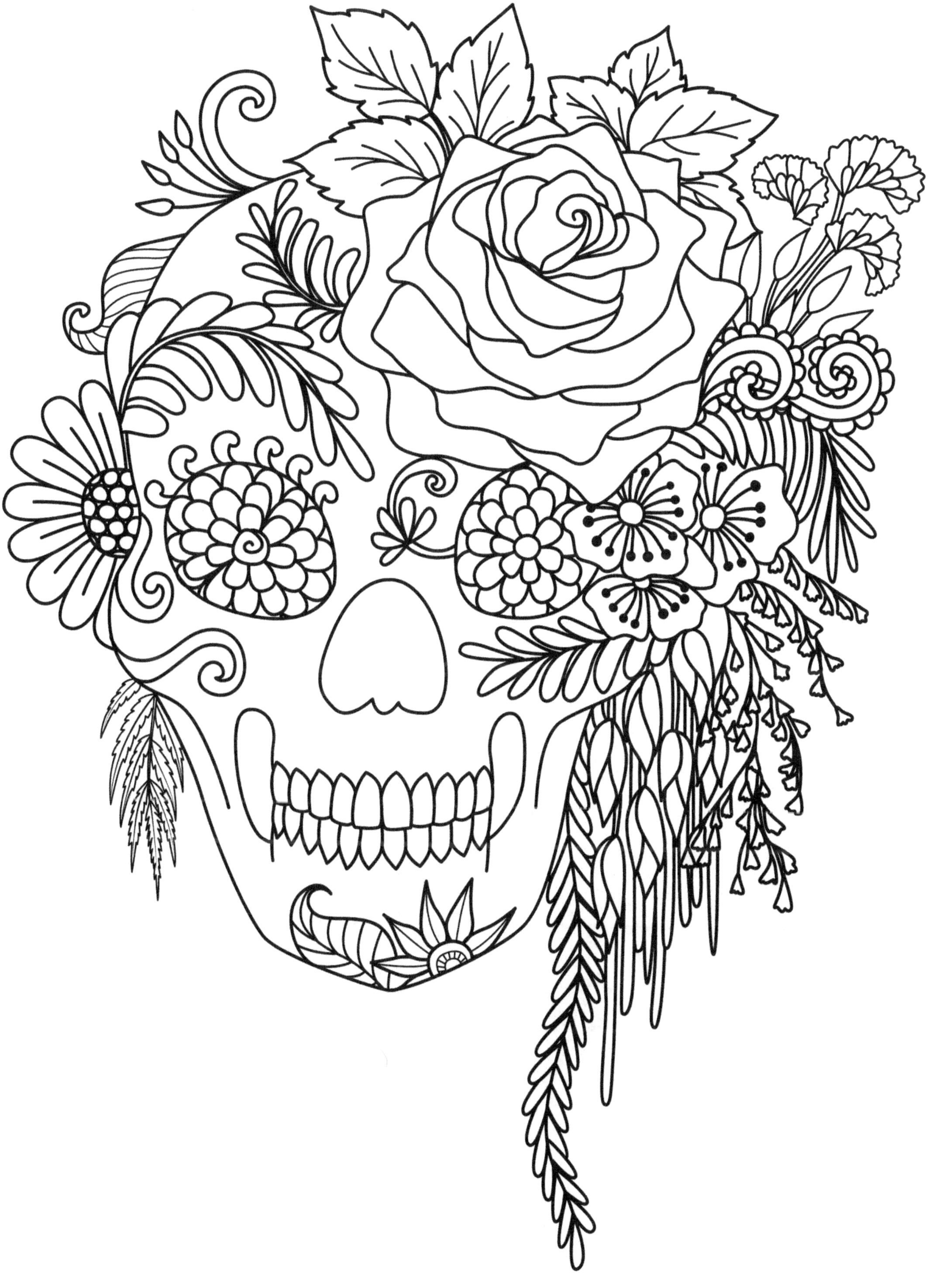

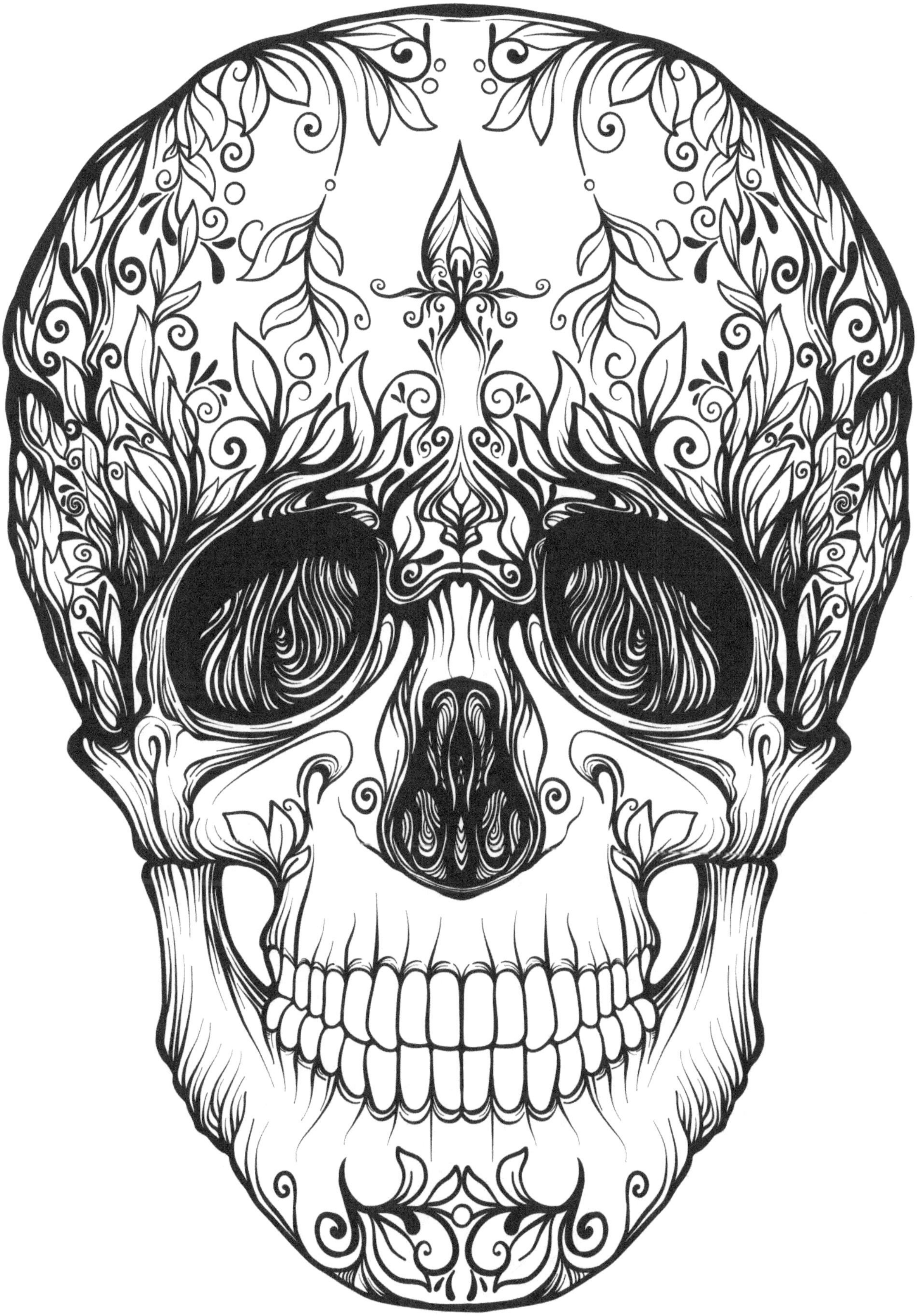

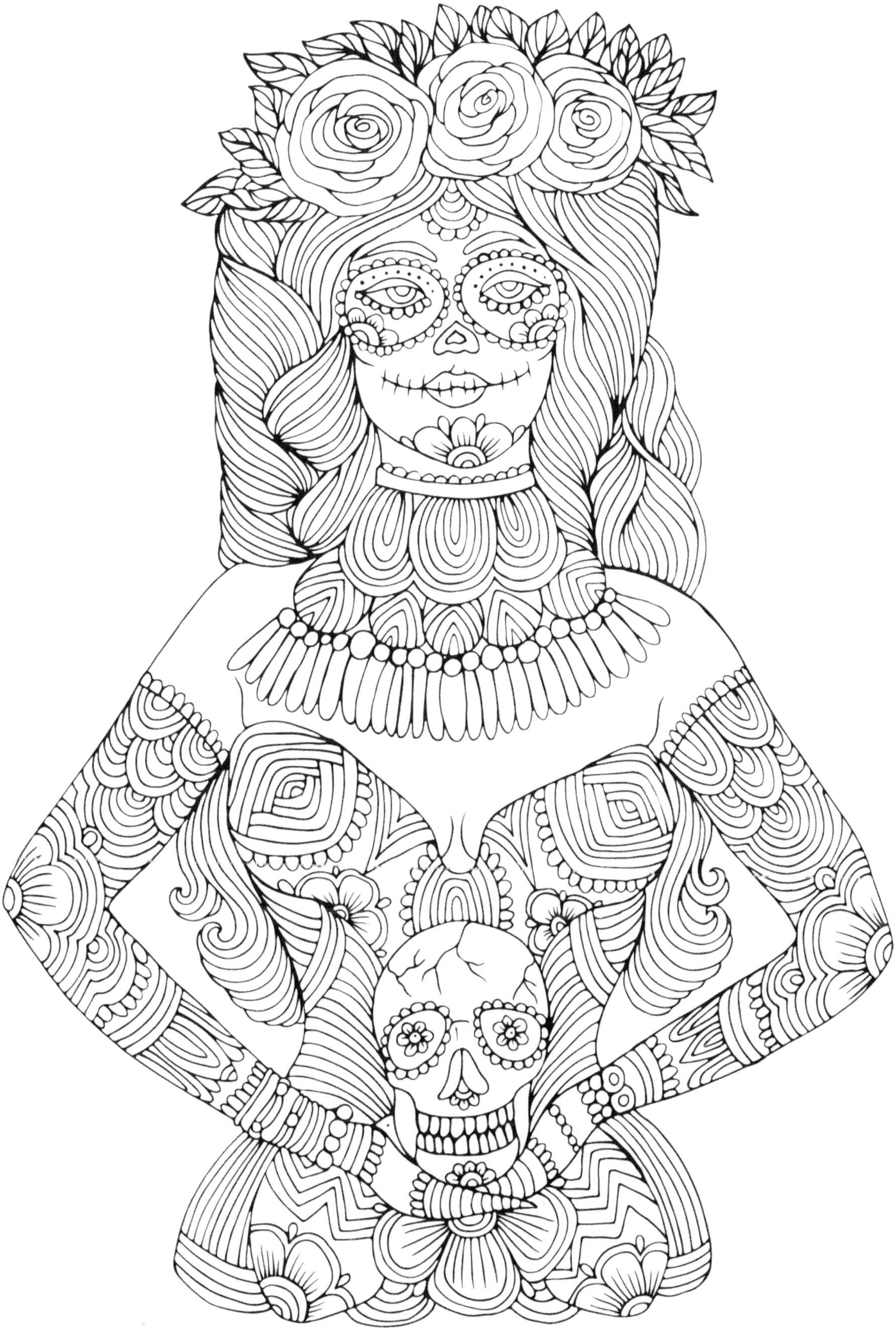

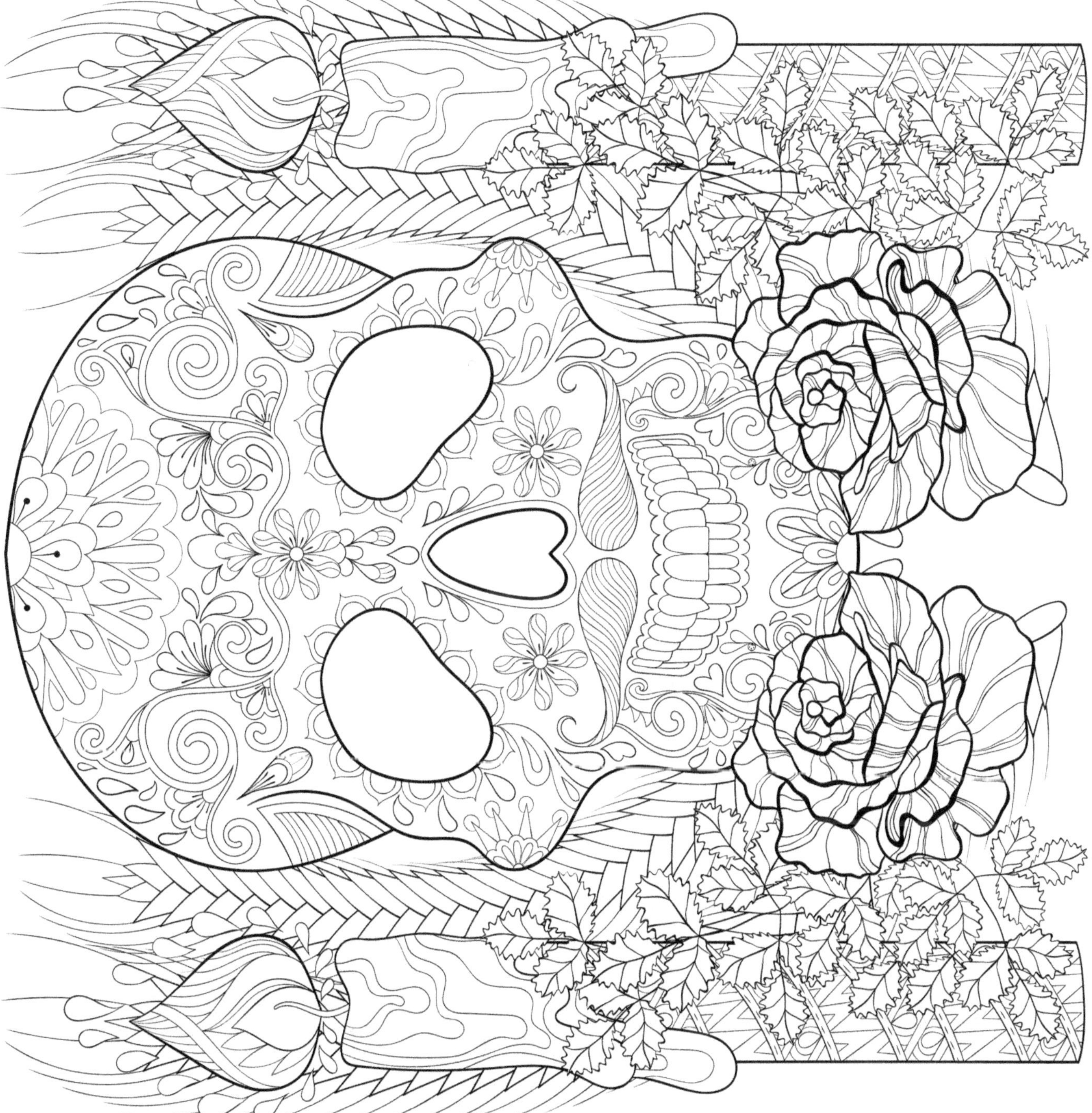

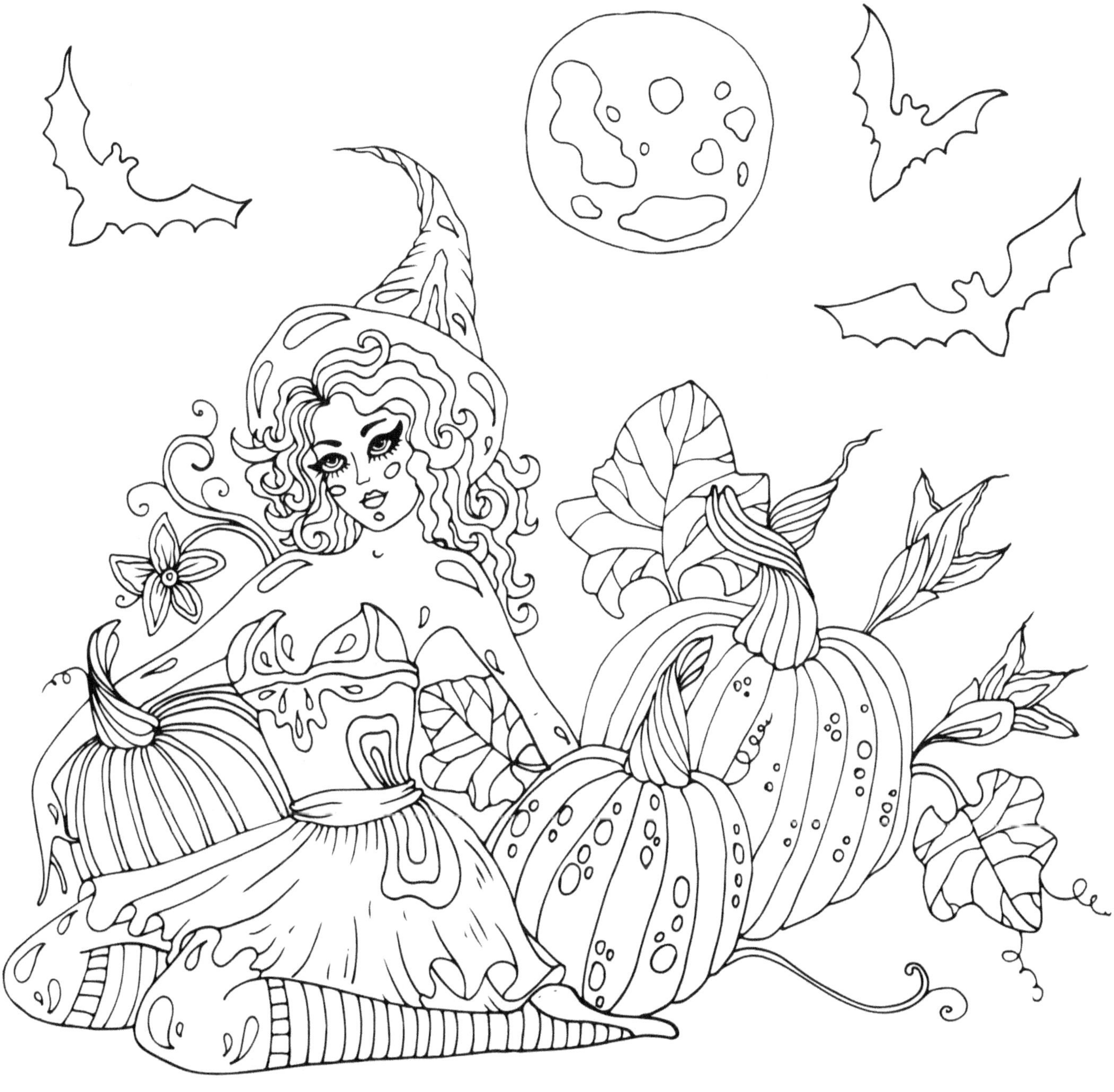

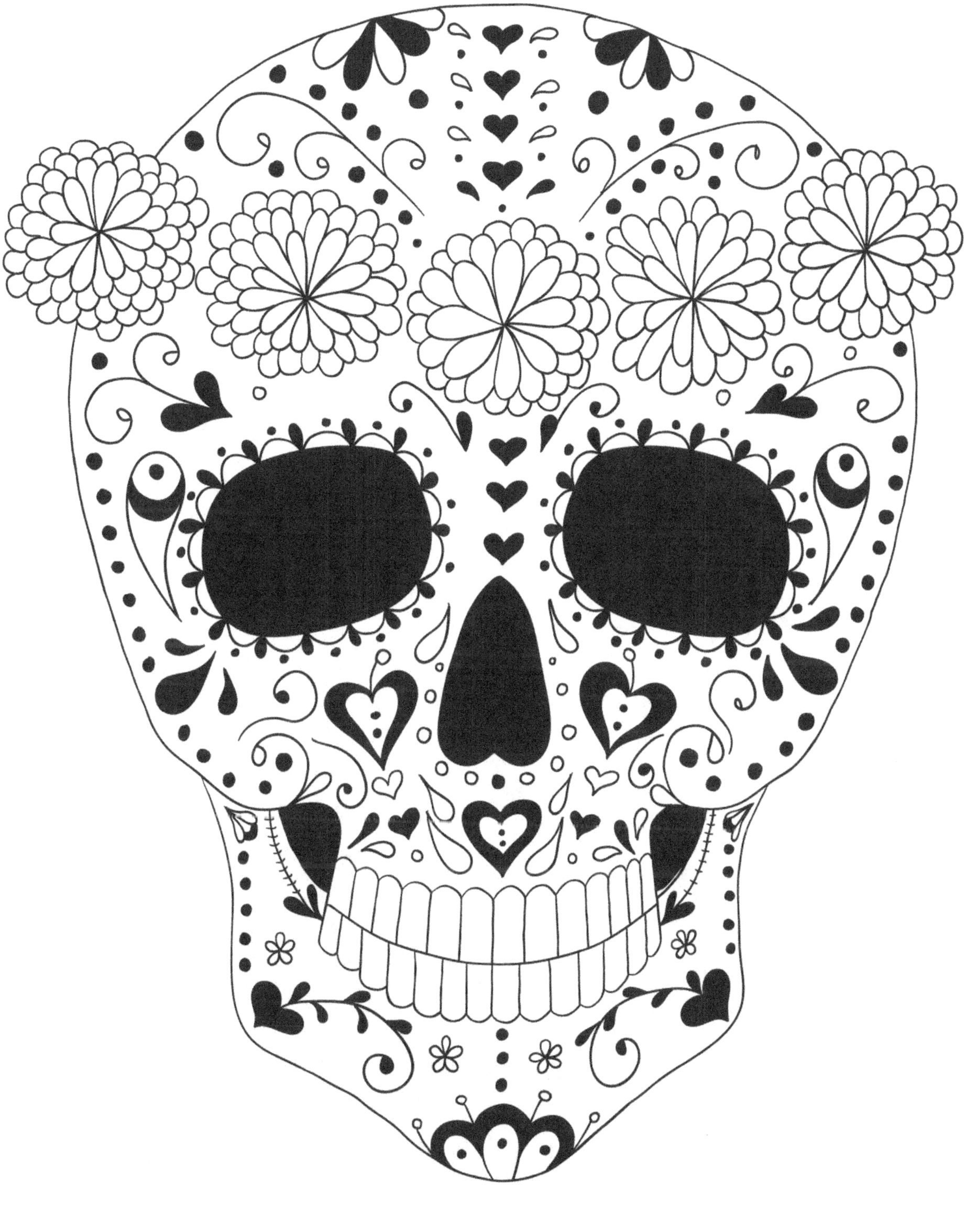

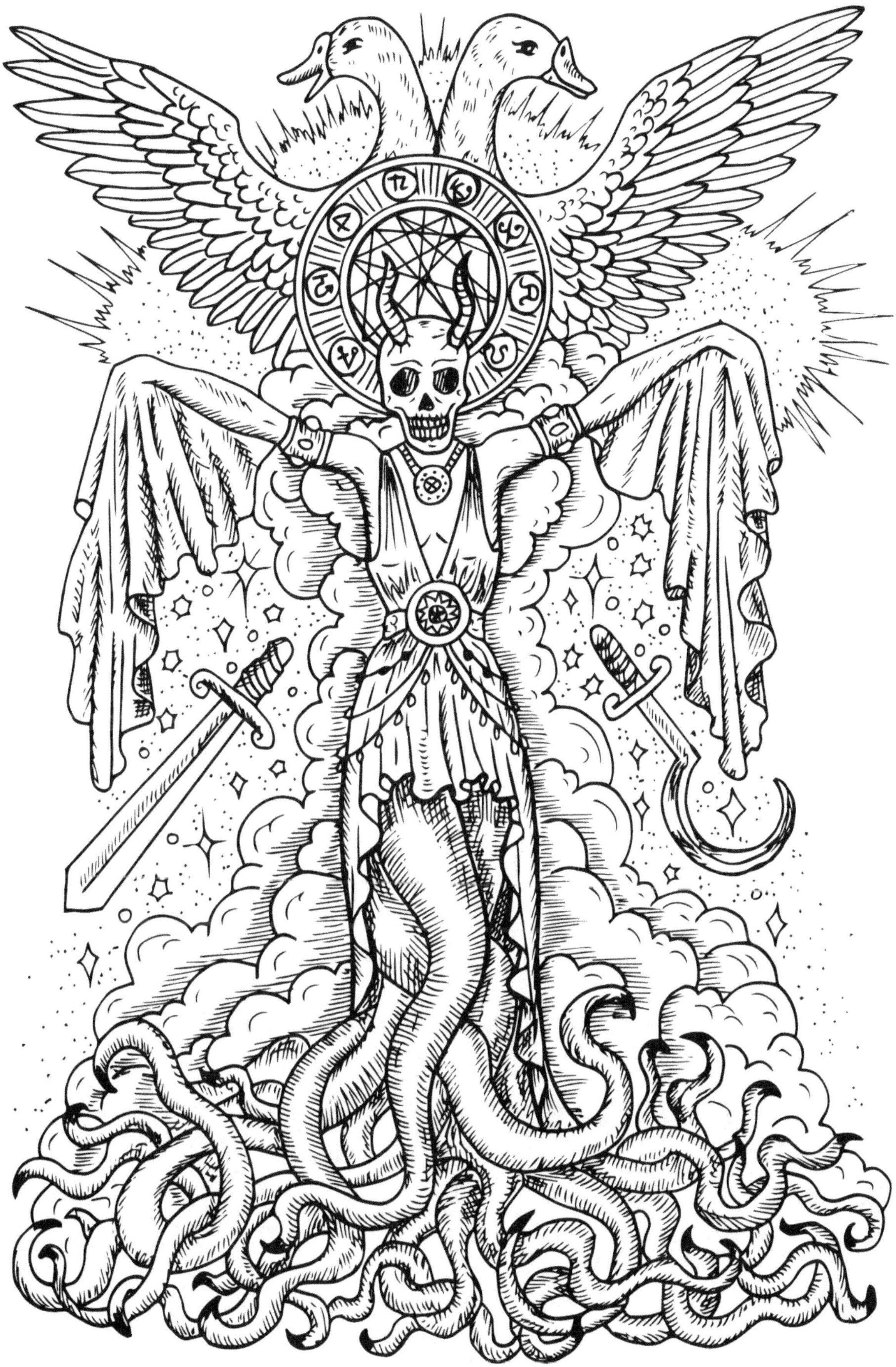

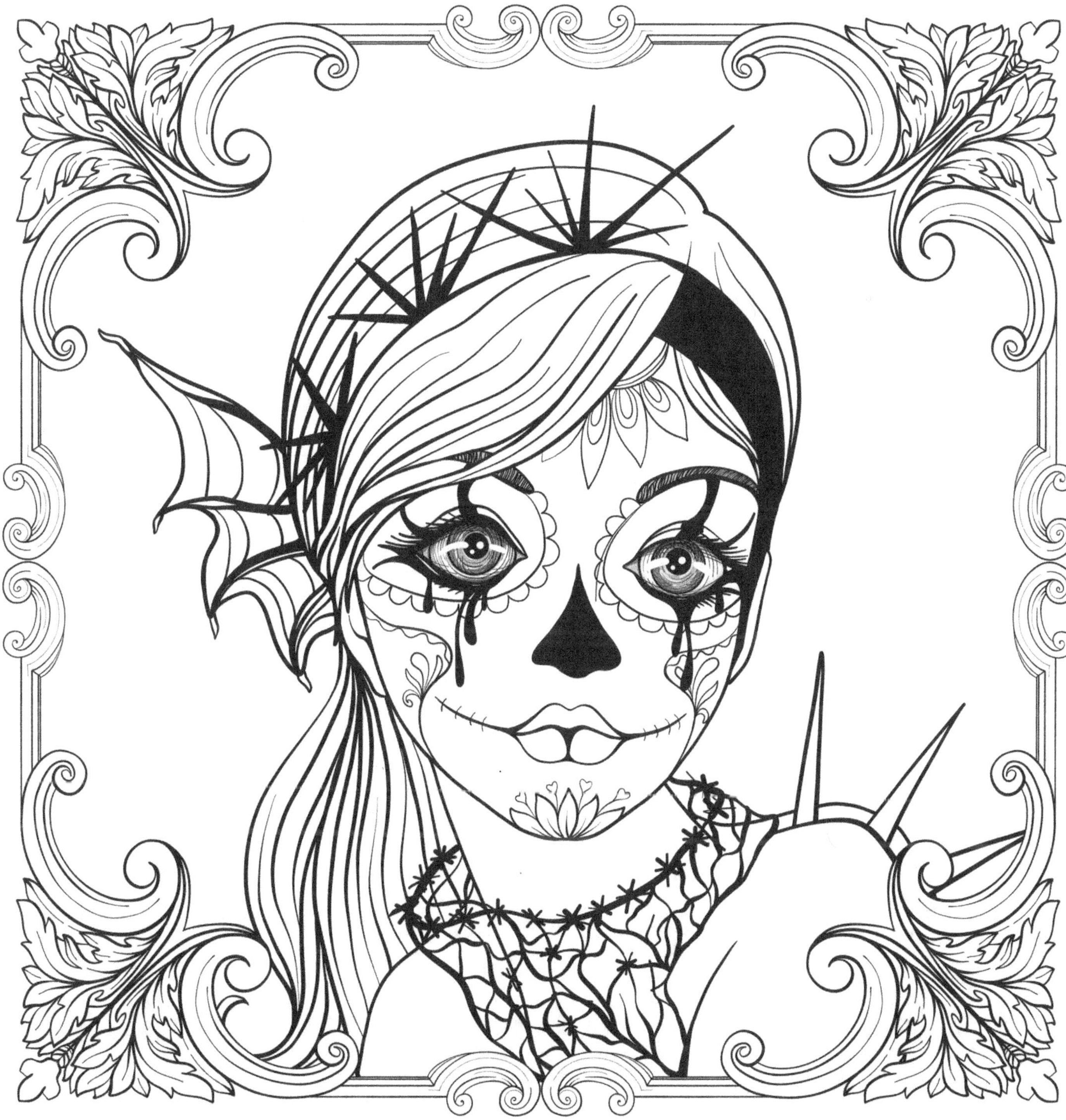

ADULTS COLORING BOOK

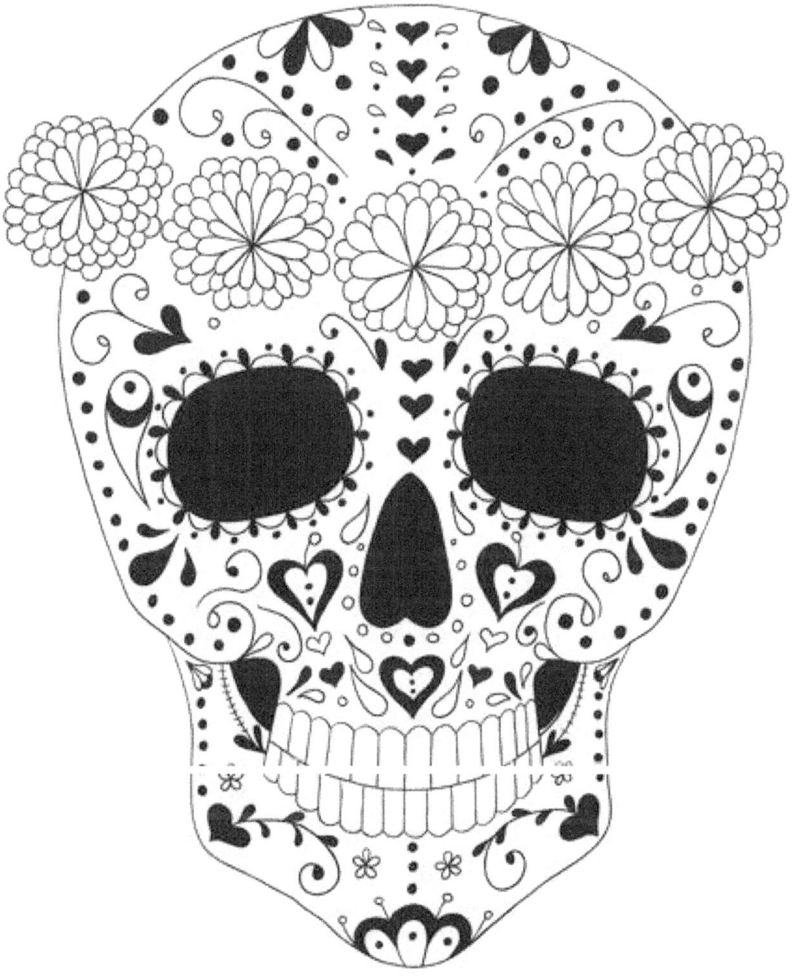

Coloring Creator

www.ingramcontent.com/pod-product-compliance
Lightning Source LLC
Chambersburg PA
CBHW062157220526
45470CB00009B/2851
* 9 7 8 1 9 7 8 2 6 7 6 2 6 *